NATIONAL GEOGRAPHIC
KiDS

PUZZLE
BOOK
SPACE
FACT-PACKED
FUN

Published by Collins
An imprint of HarperCollins Publishers
Westerhill Road
Bishopbriggs
Glasgow G64 2QT
www.harpercollins.co.uk

In association with National Geographic Partners, LLC

NATIONAL GEOGRAPHIC and the Yellow Border Design are trademarks of the
National Geographic Society, used under license.

First published 2018

ISBN 978-0-00-826769-8

10 9 8 7 6 5 4 3

Printed in Great Britain by Bell & Bain Ltd, Glasgow

If you would like to comment on any aspect of this book,
please contact us at the above address or online.
natgeokidsbooks.co.uk
collins.reference@harpercollins.co.uk

Paper from responsible sources.

Acknowledgements

Cover images

Hubble Telescope – NASA; Asteroids – Gunnar Assmy / Shutterstock.
com; Moon – Antony McAulay / Shutterstock.com; Sun – Antony
McAulay / Shutterstock.com; Space Shuttle – FotograFFF /
Shutterstock.com; Mars – Antony McAulay / Shutterstock.com;
Astronaut – Henrik Lehnerer / Shutterstock.com; Star scene –
Giovanni Benintende / Shutterstock.com; Earth – Antony McAulay /
Shutterstock.com; Rover – freestyle images / Shutterstock.com;
Saturn – Antony McAulay/Shutterstock.com

Images in order of appearance

Saturn – MarcelClemens / Shutterstock.com; Astronaut – Henrik
Lehnerer/ Shutterstock.com; Earth–Antony McAulay/Shutterstock.
com; Saturn–Antony McAulay/Shutterstock.com; Ganymede–Antony
McAulay / Shutterstock.com; Orion – Yganko / Shutterstock.com;
Astronaut–capitanoseye/Shutterstock.com; Solar System–shooarts
/ Shutterstock.com; Asteroids – Festa / Shutterstock.com; Earth –
Vadim Sadovski / Shutterstock.com; Inne Solar System – shooarts /
Shutterstock.com; Sun – Antony McAulay / Shutterstock.com;
Mercury – Antony McAulay / Shutterstock.com; Venus – Antony
McAulay/Shutterstock.com; Earth–Antony McAulay/Shutterstock.
com; Mars – Antony McAulay / Shutterstock.com; Asteroid Belt –
Gunnar Assmy / Shutterstock.com; Ceres – Nostalgia for Infinity /
Shutterstock.com; Sun – Antony McAulay / Shutterstock.com;
Mercury – Antony McAulay / Shutterstock.com; Venus – Antony
McAulay/Shutterstock.com; Earth–Antony McAulay/Shutterstock.
com; Mars–Antony McAulay/Shutterstock.com; Ceres–Nostalgia for
Infinity/Shutterstock.com; Mercury–Antony McAulay/Shutterstock.
com; Earth–Antony McAulay/Shutterstock.com; Asteroids–Gunnar
Assmy / Shutterstock.com; Saturn – MarcelClemens / Shutterstock.
com; Outer Solar System – shooarts / Shutterstock.com; Jupiter –
Antony McAulay / Shutterstock.com; Saturn – Antony McAulay /
Shutterstock.com; Uranus – Antony McAulay / Shutterstock.com;
Neptune – Antony McAulay / Shutterstock.com; Pluto – Antony
McAulay/Shutterstock.com; Kuiper Belt – Paul Fleet/Shutterstock.
com; Jupiter–Antony McAulay/Shutterstock.com; Saturn–Antony
McAulay/Shutterstock.com; Uranus–Antony McAulay/Shutterstock.
com; Neptune–Antony McAulay/Shutterstock.com; Pluto – Antony
McAulay/Shutterstock.com; Callisto–Antony McAulay/Shutterstock.
com; Europa – Antony McAulay / Shutterstock.com; Earth's Moon –
Antony McAulay / Shutterstock.com; Phobos – Antony McAulay /
Shutterstock.com; Deimos – Antony McAulay / Shutterstock.com;
Ganymede – Antony McAulay / Shutterstock.com; Callisto – Antony
McAulay/Shutterstock.com; Europa–Antony McAulay/Shutterstock.
com; Phoebe – NASA Titan – Antony McAulay / Shutterstock.com;
Hyperion – NASA Hercules – Foxyliam / Shutterstock.com; Star
background – Giovanni Benintende / Shutterstock.com; Plough –
Yganko/Shutterstock.com; Ursa Minor – Yganko/Shutterstock.com;
Canis Major – Yganko / Shutterstock.com; Orion – Yganko /
Shutterstock.com; Astronaut – capitanoseye / Shutterstock.com;
Rover – NASA Sputnik – NASA Telescope – NASA Astronaut –
capitanoseye / Shutterstock.com; Space station – Nerthuz /
Shutterstock.com; Space Shuttle – FotograFFF / Shutterstock.com;
Voyager 1 – NASA Rover – freestyle images / Shutterstock.com;
Astronaut – Fer Gregory / Shutterstock.com; Rover – sandystifler /
Shutterstock.com; Hubble Telescope – NASA Space Station – Andrey
Armyagov / Shutterstock.com; Astronaut – Andrey Armyagov /
Shutterstock.com; Space Shuttle – Vadim Sadovski / Shutterstock.
com; Rocket – Sergey Nivens/Shutterstock.com

PUZZLE BOOK

SPACE

FACT-PACKED FUN

CONTENTS

OUTER SOLAR SYSTEM   30

MOONS – NATURAL SATELLITES 50

STARS AND CONSTELLATIONS 64

SPACE EXPLORATION AND HISTORY 78

SOLUTIONS 94

SOLAR SYSTEM

Our Solar System is made up of one star, which we call the Sun, as well as eight planets, five dwarf planets, many moons, asteroids, meteoroids, comets, and a whole lot of ice, gas, and dust – it's a very busy place!

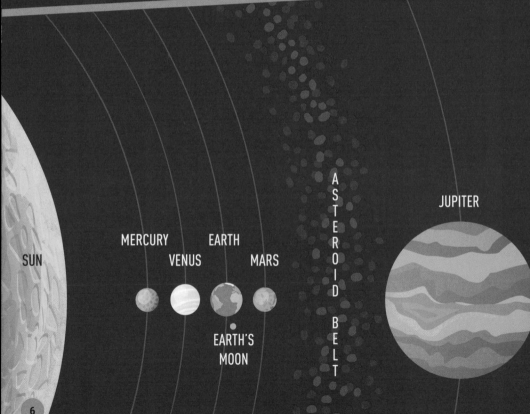

SUN

MERCURY

VENUS

EARTH

EARTH'S MOON

MARS

ASTEROID BELT

JUPITER

The **FIRST FOUR PLANETS** in the Solar System are known as the **INNER PLANETS.** The **FINAL FOUR** are known as the **OUTER PLANETS.**

SATURN

URANUS

NEPTUNE

K
U
I
P
E
R

B
E
L
T

Inner
Solar System

Read on for fun facts and puzzles from the Inner Solar System.

An **ASTEROID** that hit **EARTH** around 65 **MILLION YEARS AGO** is linked to the **EXTINCTION** of **DINOSAURS.**

INNER SOLAR SYSTEM

The Inner Solar System contains the four inner planets that are closest to the Sun: Mercury, Venus, Earth and Mars. Also known as the terrestrial planets, they have solid, rocky surfaces and in this way they are similar to Earth. Don't be fooled though, they are all very different from one another! Our Moon is one of only three moons in the Inner Solar System; the other two orbit Mars.

SUN

Although **MERCURY** is closer to the **SUN**, **VENUS** is the **WARMEST** planet. **HEAT** is **TRAPPED** under its **THICK** and toxic **ATMOSPHERE**.

MERCURY

VENUS

EARTH

MARS

EARTH'S
MOON

ASTEROID BELT

CROSSWORDS

Launch the spacecraft to the Sun by solving the cryptic clues below. Answers have the same amount of letters as the number in brackets. Can you work out the Inner Solar System keyword using the letters in the shaded squares? See if you are right by flicking to page 94.

The **SUN** is so big that you could fit every other object in our **SOLAR SYSTEM** inside it! (Or about **1,300,000 EARTHS!**)

Across
4. Meal eaten outdoors (6)
6. Turn over and over (4)
7. Organ you see with (3)
8. Not hot (4)
9. Additionally (4)
10. Opposite of in (3)
11. Assist (4)
12. Continent where you find England and France (6)

Down
1. Dots shine (anagram) (9)
2. You put a letter in this before posting it (8)
3. Device used to study stars (9)
5. Any animal (8)

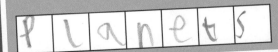

The **Sun** is the scorching hot star of our Solar System. Even though it is 150 million kilometres away, it gives us heat and light, sustaining all life on Earth.

Across

4 E.g. Asia or Europe (9)
6 Boy's name (3)
8 Strong feeling of annoyance (5)
9 Sweet and sticky liquid (5)
10 Item of neckwear often worn with a suit (3)
12 Person in a story (9)

Down

1 Where you live (4)
2 Vanish from sight (9)
3 Heaviness (6)
5 Number in a trio (5)
6 Simple (5)
7 Country whose capital is Oslo (6)
11 Thought or suggestion (4)

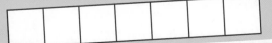

SUDOKUS

Solve the sudokus to launch the spacecraft to Mercury.
Fill in the blank squares so that numbers 1 to 6 appear once in each row,
column and 3x2 box. See if you are right by flicking to page 94.

2	4	6	3		
1	5	3			
4			6	7	3
6		5			
				2	4
				3	

Mercury is the closest planet to the Sun, which
makes it the hottest place to be... right? Well,
although one side of Mercury is extremely hot, there
is no atmosphere to keep the heat in, which means
the other side is very cold. Mercury is also the
smallest planet, not much larger than our moon.

	2		4		
			3	6	
				1	
	4				3
	1	3			
2		4	1	3	

If you were on **MERCURY,** the **SUN** would appear three times larger in the sky than it does on **EARTH,** and a whole lot **BRIGHTER!**

Wordsearches

Search the Solar Sytem to find the space words. Look left to right, up and down to find the words listed in the boxes below. See if you are right by flicking to page 94.

asteroid
comet
gravity
light
meteoroid
moons
orbit
planets
star
Sun

i	r	b	r	o	r	b	i	t	a
l	r	l	x	l	h	q	p	a	e
u	l	p	l	a	n	e	t	s	n
m	i	a	g	r	a	v	i	t	y
u	g	c	j	a	j	s	n	e	r
e	h	o	k	a	a	t	m	r	k
p	t	m	t	e	a	a	o	o	a
u	m	e	t	e	o	r	o	i	d
e	l	t	r	s	o	o	n	d	p
e	l	p	t	r	a	o	s	u	n

Venus is one of Earth's neighbours, but it is very different from Earth! Covered in volcanoes and lava flows, Venus is the hottest planet in the Solar System. It is also the brightest object in the night sky after the Sun and our Moon.

k	u	z	e	p	r	o	c	k	y
s	t	t	m	t	y	e	r	t	a
q	t	v	e	o	m	b	a	t	b
q	m	a	r	s	c	j	t	k	x
v	o	l	c	a	n	o	e	s	p
e	v	l	u	k	e	a	r	t	h
n	c	e	r	e	s	d	s	p	p
u	t	y	y	t	l	b	d	x	s
s	t	s	o	l	i	d	m	b	t
l	o	e	j	i	m	o	h	l	e

- Ceres
- craters
- Earth
- Mars
- Mercury
- rocky
- solid
- valleys
- Venus
- volcanoes

VENUS was named after the ROMAN GODDESS of love because of its brightness and beauty in the night SKY.

WORD JUMBLES

Return to Earth by rearranging the jumbled letters to form Earth-related words. See if you are right by flicking to page 94.

T A H E E S R P O M

S O N A E C

Y R T I G V A

M E N L T A

U C T R S

70 per cent of the **EARTH'S** surface is covered by **OCEANS.** That's a lot of **WATER!**

Earth is a very special planet: it is our home, and the only planet in the Universe known to support life! Sheltered by a protective atmosphere, the Earth is home to trees, plants and animals that are all able to live and breathe thanks to an abundance of water and breathable air.

MAZES

Work your way around the mazes on Mars until you reach the top of Olympus Mons. See if you are right by flicking to page 95.

MARS is home to the tallest **MOUNTAIN** in the **SOLAR SYSTEM, OLYMPUS MONS,** which is 2.5 times **TALLER** than **EARTH'S** biggest **MOUNTAIN, MOUNT EVEREST.** But watch out, it's a **VOLCANO,** too!

Mars is Earth's slightly closer neighbour. Also called the red planet, Mars was named after the Roman god of war because of its blood red colour. Regular dust storms mean that the surface of Mars is covered in a thick layer of red dust.

Word wheels

Can you work out the space objects in the three word wheels?
See if you are right by flicking to page 95.

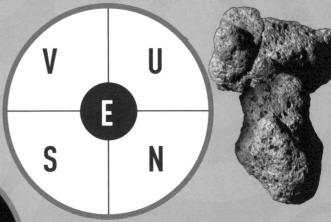

V U
E
S N

ASTEROID FLORENCE swept past Earth in September 2017. **ASTRONOMERS** were surprised to find that it had not one, but **TWO MOONS** in **ORBIT!**

The planets of our Solar System aren't alone in orbiting the Sun – they are joined by millions of lumps of rock that are like mini-planets. These space rocks are called asteroids, and the Asteroid Belt is a huge concentration of them, in orbit between Mars and Jupiter, separating the inner and outer planets.

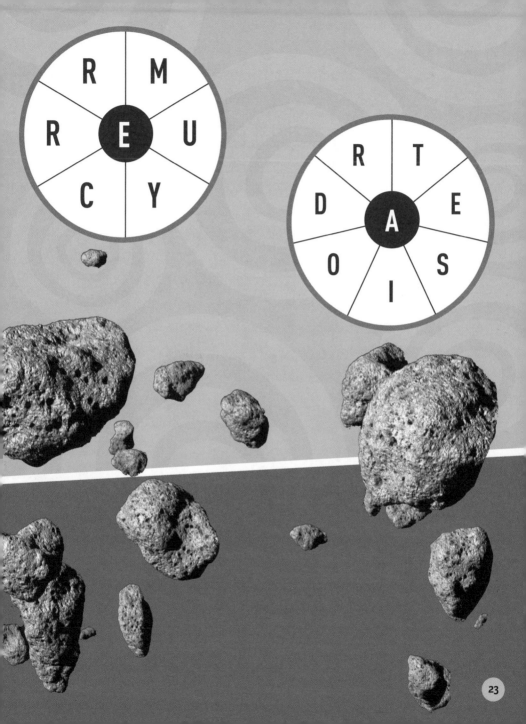

23

Codewords

Can you complete these super-tricky codewords? Each letter of the alphabet is represented by a number. Some have been given to start you off. Fill the grid with words and once it is full, see if you can work out the codeword using the shaded squares. See if you are right by flicking to page 95.

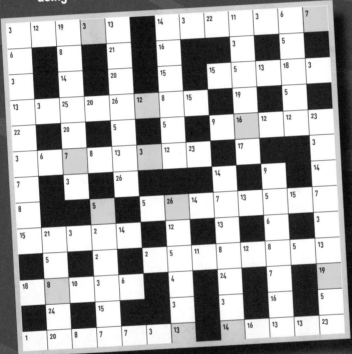

1	2	3	4	5	6	7	8	9	10	11	12	13
Q		E		A				I	J	X		R

14	15	16	17	18	19	20	21	22	23	24	25	26
			W	V	D			G				

(8,4)

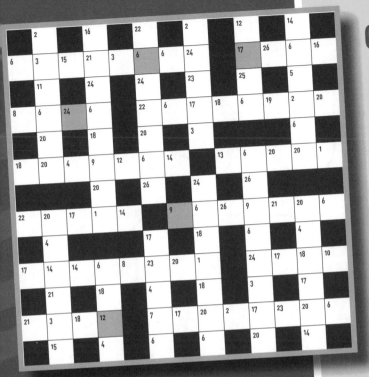

Ceres is by far the largest object in the Asteroid Belt, measuring about 950 kilometres in diameter. Because of its size, gravity has rounded it into a sphere, and that's why it is classed as a dwarf planet. Amongst millions of asteroids, it is the only minor planet in the Asteroid Belt.

CLOSE UP

Match the mind-boggling magnifications to the named pictures opposite.
See if you are right by flicking to page 95.

1

2

3

4

5

6

Sun

1

Mercury

2

Venus

3

Earth

4

Mars

5

6 Ceres

GUESS WHAT?

Can you guess the answers to the Inner Solar System questions below?
Check your guesses by flicking to page 95.

1. How many inner planets are there?
   - a) 1
   - b) 4
   - c) 8

2. The Asteroid Belt is found beyond the orbit of which planet?
   - a) Mercury
   - b) Earth
   - c) Mars

3. Which is the smallest planet in the Solar System?
   - a) Mercury
   - b) Earth
   - c) Jupiter

4. Which is the only planet known to have life?
   - a) Earth
   - b) Venus
   - c) Saturn

5. What is the largest object in the Asteroid Belt?
   - a) Ceres
   - b) Series
   - C) Sirius

6. Who is the planet Mars named after?
  a) The Roman god of love
  b) The Roman god of peace
  c) The Roman god of war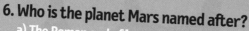

7. How long is a year on Mercury?
  a) 11 Earth days
  b) 88 Earth days
  c) 888 Earth days

8. How many moons does Venus have?
  a) 0
  b) 2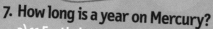
  c) 4

9. What is the name of the third planet from the Sun?
  a) Earth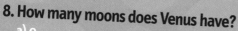
  b) Mars
  c) Jupiter

10. Mars has a mountain that rises 25 kilometres above the surrounding land. What is it called?
  a) Olympus Mens
  b) Olympus Mons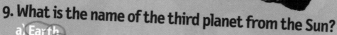
  c) Olympus Mans

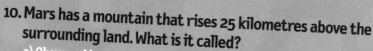
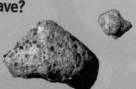

Outer Solar System

Discover fun facts and puzzles on the Outer Solar System in this chapter.

SATURN'S RINGS extend 282,000 **KILOMETRES** out into space and are **10–30 METRES THICK.**

OUTER SOLAR SYSTEM

The four planets of the Outer Solar System are Jupiter, Saturn, Uranus and Neptune. Much larger than the inner planets, Jupiter and Saturn are made mostly of gas, which is why they are sometimes known as the Gas Giants. Neptune and Uranus are known as the Water or Ice Giants. Saturn is famous for its rings, but the other three outer planets have rings, too.

JUPITER

The **OUTER PLANETS** have many **MOONS**: altogether around **170** have been counted so far, but **ASTRONOMERS** are still discovering more!

SCIENTISTS believe that, deep within their atmospheres, **URANUS** and **NEPTUNE** rain diamonds!

SATURN

URANUS

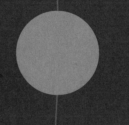

NEPTUNE

K
U
I
P
E
R

B
E
L
T

CROSSWORDS

Crack the crosswords to launch the mission to Jupiter by solving the cryptic clues below.
Answers have the same amount of letters as the number in brackets.
Can you work out the Outer Solar System keyword using the letters in the shaded squares?
See if you are right by flicking to page 96.

JUPITER has an area called the Great Red Spot, which is thought to be a gigantic **STORM** that has been raging on for at least **150 YEARS!**

Across
1 Draw special attention to; best part (9)
5 Put briefly into liquid (3)
7 African country (7)
8 On the ___ : about to happen (7)
11 Large flightless Australian bird (3)
12 Exploding star (9)

Down
1 Small mammals with spiny coats (9)
2 Spaces or intervals (4)
3 Female child (4)
4 Large hairy spider (9)
6 Surprise greatly (5)
9 Sloping surface (4)
10 Finding ___ : film about a clownfish (4)

Jupiter is also known as the giant planet. Why? Because it's the biggest planet in the Solar System, at more than 300 times the size of Earth! As if that wasn't impressive enough, Jupiter also has the most moons of any planet in our Solar System, with at least 67 discovered so far.

Across

1 Crisis (9)
5 Animal with a snout (3)
7 Put an idea forward for consideration (7)
8 E.g. Maths or English (7)
11 Primary colour (3)
12 Very (9)

Down

1 Opposite of cheap (9)
2 Chickens lay these (4)
3 Pleasant (4)
4 The day before today (9)
6 Have the same opinion; concur (5)
9 Type of shoe (4)
10 E.g. oak or sycamore (4)

SUDOKUS

Send a spacecraft to Saturn by solving the sudokus. Fill in the blank squares so that numbers 1 to 6 appear once in each row, column and 3x2 box. See if you are right by flicking to page 96.

4			5		
	6		2		
		4			6
5		6			
		2		1	
		3			5

SATURN has seven groups of rings which orbit it at different speeds. They are made of billions of pieces of ice and rock that range in size from dust particles to mountain-sized.

				6	4
					5
	4		1		
		3		2	
6					
3	1	5	6		2

SATURN'S DAYS are less than **HALF** as long as ours: only **10 HOURS** and **14 MINUTES.** But its **YEARS** are more than **29 TIMES LONGER.**

Wordsearches

Search the Solar Sytem to find the space words. Look left to right,
up and down to find the words listed in the boxes below.
See if you are right by flicking to page 96.

cold
Gas Giants
huge
Jupiter
moons
Neptune
red spot
rings
Saturn
Uranus

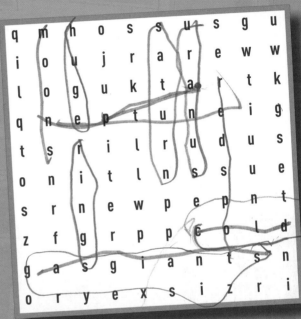

q	m	h	o	s	s	s	u	s	g	u
i	o	u	j	r	a	r	e	w	w
l	o	g	u	k	t	a	r	t	k
q	n	e	p	t	u	n	e	i	g
t	s	r	i	l	r	u	d	u	s
o	n	i	t	l	n	s	s	u	e
s	r	n	e	w	p	e	p	n	t
z	f	g	r	p	p	c	o	l	d
g	a	s	g	i	a	n	t	s	n
o	r	y	e	x	s	i	z	r	i

The icy giant **Uranus** is very cold and windy. Also called the sideways
planet, it appears to be rolling around the Sun on its side. This unusual
angle means that the seasons on Uranus are extreme, with half of the
planet being plunged into a dark winter for 21 years at a time.

w	p	s	i	a	p	e	t	u	s
r	p	e	c	a	t	h	e	b	e
z	l	s	h	b	r	y	b	t	j
p	b	c	a	i	s	p	u	i	p
h	y	d	r	o	g	e	n	t	l
o	p	j	o	o	m	r	o	a	u
e	b	q	n	l	i	i	o	n	t
b	f	s	l	r	m	o	b	i	o
e	z	m	i	r	a	n	d	a	o
l	v	w	e	k	s	v	u	l	f

Charon
hydrogen
Hyperion
Iapetus
Mimas
Miranda
Phoebe
Pluto
Thebe
Titania

URANUS is named after the GREEK GOD of the SKY. However, the ASTRONOMER that first discovered the planet wanted to name it after KING GEORGE.

39

MAZES

Work your way around the mazes on Neptune until you reach the exit.
See if you are right by flicking to page 97.

See if you are right by flicking to page 97.

NEPTUNE
has an average
TEMPERATURE
of **−214°C** on its
SURFACE but
7000°C at its
CORE.

Neptune is the planet furthest from the Sun, our Solar System's only source of heat and light, so it is also the darkest, coldest, and windiest planet in the Solar System. Neptune is deep blue in colour, which probably explains why it was named after the Roman god of the sea.

WORD JUMBLES

Send a spacecraft to Pluto by rearranging the jumbled letters to form space-related words. See if you are right by flicking to page 97.

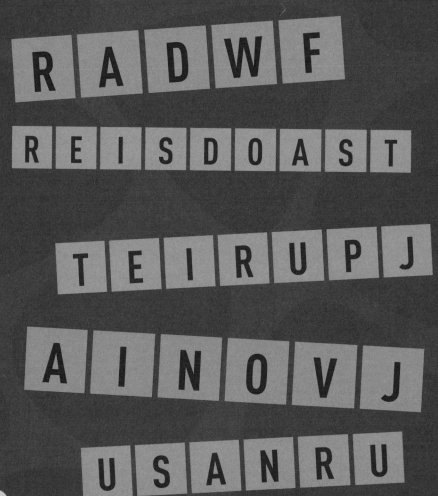

R A D W F

R E I S D O A S T

T E I R U P J

A I N O V J

U S A N R U

For a long time, **Pluto** was considered the ninth planet of our Solar System, but in 2006 it was reclassified as a dwarf planet. Pluto is usually covered in ice, but for some parts of its orbit the ice melts a little and a thin nitrogen atmosphere is formed.

PLUTO is so far away from the Sun that its orbit takes a very long time – one year on Pluto is about as long as **248 YEARS** on **EARTH!**

Codewords

Can you complete these super-tricky codewords? Each letter of the alphabet is represented by a number. Some have been given to start you off. Fill the grid with words and once it is full, see if you can work out the codeword using the shaded squares. See if you are right by flicking to page 97.

Letter key:

1	2	3	4	5	6	7	8	9	10	11	12	13
P		G	D	H			A			T	R	

14	15	16	17	18	19	20	21	22	23	24	25	26
E							V		Y			C

Codeword answer: (6,4)

The **Kuiper Belt** is a concentration of millions of rocky, icy objects that orbit our Sun outside the orbit of Pluto. These objects may possibly hold clues about the origins of our Solar System, but they are so far away that they are very difficult for astronomers to see and study.

1	2	3	4	5	6	7	8	9	10	11	12	13
E				T		L	O	H	H			D

14	15	16	17	18	19	20	21	22	23	24	25	26
		S			Q			F	A	P		

Objects in the **KUIPER BELT** are thought to be leftover mess from the beginning of our **SOLAR SYSTEM** that has been swept out to the edges by the gravity of large planets.

CLOSE UP

Match the mind-boggling magnifications to the named pictures opposite. See if you are right by flicking to page 97.

1

2

3

4

5

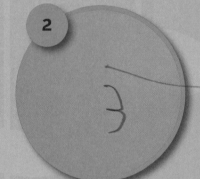

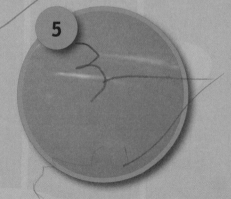
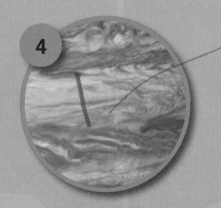

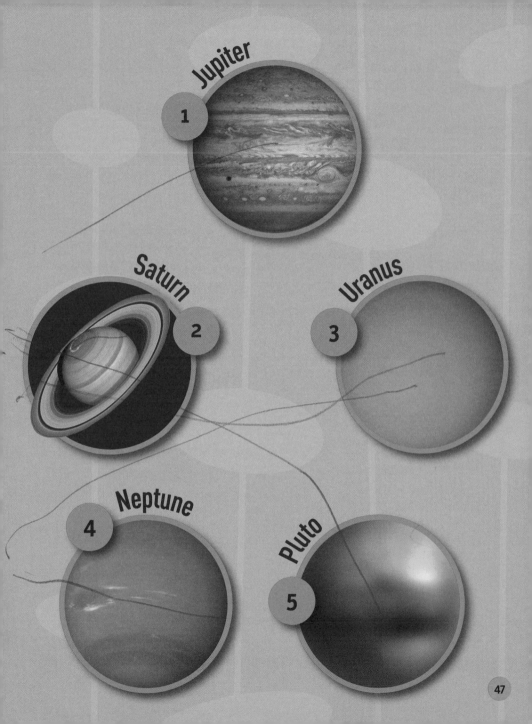

Jupiter

1

Saturn

2

Uranus

3

Neptune

4

Pluto

5

47

GUESS WHAT?

Can you guess the answers to the Outer Solar System questions below?
Check your guesses by flicking to page 97.

1. What are Jupiter and Saturn sometimes known as?
   a) Rock Giants
   b) Gas Giants
   c) Liquid Giants

2. Which is the second-largest planet?
   a) Saturn
   b) Neptune
   c) Venus

3. Which of these is a famous feature of Jupiter?
   a) Great Green Spot
   b) Great Blue Spot
   c) Great Red Spot

4. How many moons does Jupiter have?
   a) Less than 20
   b) Less than 40
   c) More than 60

5. One of Jupiter's moons is the largest in the Solar System. What is it called?
   a) Thebe
   b) Callisto
   c) Ganymede

6. What is Saturn mainly made of?
   a) Lithium
   b) Hydrogen
   c) Carbon

7. What is the name of Saturn's largest moon, which is the only moon known to have a dense atmosphere?
   a) Phoebe
   b) Titan
   c) Mimas

8. What is the name of the seventh planet from the Sun?
   a) Uranus
   b) Pluto
   c) Mars

9. Who is the planet Neptune named after?
   a) The Roman god of the sea
   b) The Roman god of lightning
   c) The Roman god of destiny

10. Which of these is known as a dwarf planet?
    a) Pluto
    b) Mercury
    c) Earth

Word wheels

Can you work out the planets in the three word wheels?
See if you are right by flicking to page 97.

Moons
Natural satellites

Learn about marvellous moons with fun facts and puzzles in this chapter.

CALLISTO, one of **SATURN'S MOONS,** is the **MOST CRATERED** object in the Solar System. It is the Solar System's **THIRD LARGEST MOON** with a **DIAMETER** of over **4,800 KM** and is nearly the same size as Mercury.

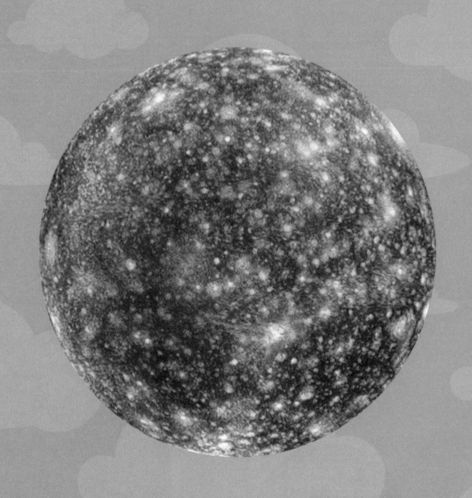

MOONS

Our Solar System is packed with hundreds of moons. These moons, also called satellites, come in a variety of shapes and sizes.

The Inner Solar System is home to three moons – one for Earth and two for Mars. Mercury and Venus have no moons.

The planets of the Outer Solar System have many moons.

Let's look at some of these moons more closely...

Dwarf planet **PLUTO** is **SMALLER** THAN **EARTH'S MOON** but has **FIVE MOONS** of its own.

JUPITER'S moon, **EUROPA,** is thought to have a **SALT-WATER OCEAN** – just like Earth.

CROSSWORDS

Crack the crosswords to land safely on the Moon by solving the cryptic clues below.
Answers have the same amount of letters as the number in brackets.
Can you work out the moon keyword using the letters in the shaded squares?
See if you are right by flicking to page 98.

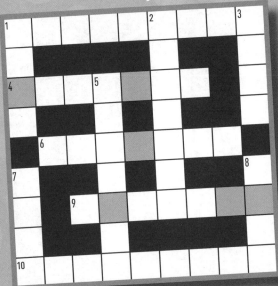

The first person to set foot on the **MOON** was **NEIL ARMSTRONG,** in **1969,** who famously said *'That's one small step for man, one giant leap for mankind'.*

Across

1 Day before Thursday (9)
4 Help and assist (7)
6 Item blown by a referee (7)
9 Appliance (7)
10 Exciting trip (9)

Down

1 Opposite of east (4)
2 Make something longer by pulling it (7)
3 Period of 365 days (4)
5 Opposite of public (7)
7 Space agency of United States of America (4)
8 Where you are right now (4)

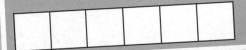

Luna, Cynthia, Selene – there are many names for our **Moon,** but whatever you want to call it, there's no denying that it's Earth's closest companion within the Solar System. As **Earth** orbits the Sun, the Moon comes with us, orbiting our planet at the same time. Earth's Moon is the only other place in the Solar System that humans have visited, so far...

Across
4 Way of doing something (6)
6 You use these to hear (4)
7 Fix; repair (4)
8 Talk to your friends (4)
9 Border (4)
10 No person (6)

Down
1 Also known as 'hump day' (9)
2 Kids (8)
3 You might spread this on toast (9)
5 Give details about (8)

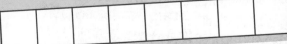

SUDOKUS

Solve the sudokus to launch the test flight to Phobos.
Fill in the blank squares so that numbers 1 to 6 appear
once in each row, column and 3x2 box.
See if you are right by flicking to page 98.

	4				
	2		4	3	
	3				5
1					
2	6	5		1	4
				2	

Mars' moons Phobos and Deimos are among some of the
smallest moons in the Solar System. Like Earth's moon, both
have lumpy, dusty surfaces covered in craters. Both moons orbit
quite close to the Martian surface, so if you were to stand on
one, Mars would take up a lot of the sky view.

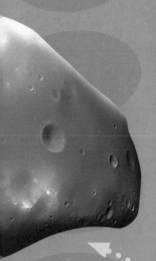

Phobos

6			5	2	
	6			5	
	3			4	
	1	4			3
	2				

SCIENTISTS think that in the future one of MARS' moons could be used as a BASE for ASTRONAUTS to stay at while they OBSERVE the RED PLANET.

Deimos

Wordsearches

Search the Solar Sytem to find the moon-related terms.
Look left to right, up and down to find the words listed in the boxes below.
See if you are right by flicking to page 98.

atmosphere
core ✓
crust ✓
eclipse
full moon
mantle
mountains
new moon
oceans
water

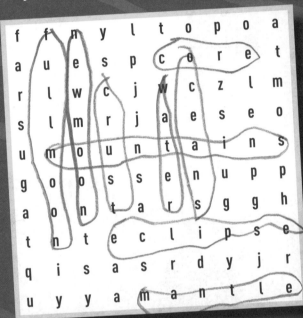

f f n y l t o p o a
a u e s p c o r e t
r l w c j w c z l m
s l m r j a e s e o
u m o u n t a i n s
g o o s s e n u p p
a o n t a r s g g h
t n t e c l i p s e
q i s a s r d y j r
u y y a m a n t l e

Jupiter has its very own Solar System, with at least 67 moons in orbit. As well as being the biggest planet, Jupiter also has the biggest moon – Ganymede, which is nearly twice the size of Earth's moon!

Ganymede

u	t	s	w	j	m	o	o	n	v
r	h	e	a	d	e	n	b	d	u
m	a	u	w	i	t	o	e	a	d
a	b	r	a	c	h	a	r	o	n
e	r	o	u	e	v	d	o	f	a
u	y	p	t	i	t	a	n	r	r
d	c	a	l	l	i	s	t	o	i
s	s	g	a	n	y	m	e	d	e
r	b	b	t	r	i	t	o	n	l
n	r	i	w	s	x	q	i	t	r

Ariel
Callisto
Charon
Europa
Ganymede
Moon
Oberon
Rhea
Titan
Triton

Callisto

All of **JUPITER'S MOONS** are like very different little worlds. One moon named Io is home to over **400** active **VOLCANOES,** which makes it the most active object in the entire **SOLAR SYSTEM!**

Europa

MAZES

Work your way around the mazes on Saturn's moons until you reach the exit. See if you are right by flicking to page 99.

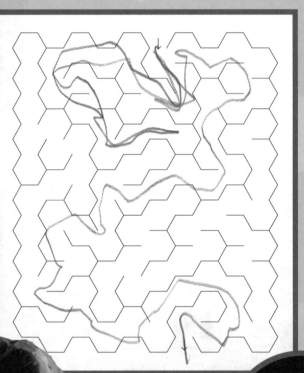

PHOEBE is a rebellious moon, as it orbits **SATURN** in the **OPPOSITE DIRECTION** to most other **MOONS.**

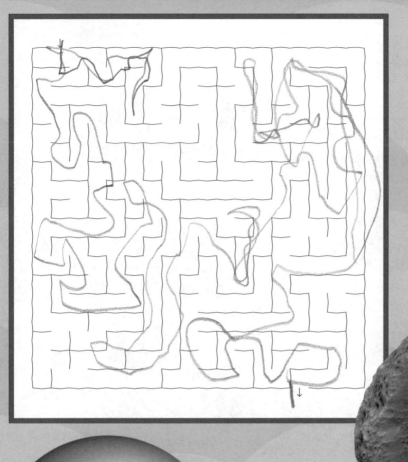

Hyperion

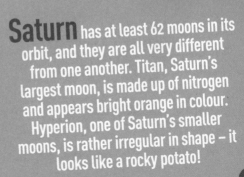

Titan

Saturn has at least 62 moons in its orbit, and they are all very different from one another. Titan, Saturn's largest moon, is made up of nitrogen and appears bright orange in colour. Hyperion, one of Saturn's smaller moons, is rather irregular in shape – it looks like a rocky potato!

GUESS WHAT?

Can you guess the answers to the moon questions below?
Check your guesses by flicking to page 99.

1. How many moons does the planet Mars have?
   a) 0
   b) 2
   c) 4

2. How long ago is Earth's moon thought to have formed?
   a) About 4.5 million years ago
   b) About 45 million years ago
   c) About 4.5 billion years ago

3. How long does it take for the Moon to orbit the Earth?
   a) About 17 days
   b) About 27 days
   c) About 37 days

4. With over 400 active volcanoes, which moon of Jupiter is the most geologically active object in the Solar System?
   a) Io
   b) Jo
   C) Mo

5. Which of these is a moon of Jupiter?
   a) Europa
   b) Phobos
   c) Helene

6. Which is Saturn's second-largest moon?
   a) Rhea
   b) Lea
   c) Shea

7. Saturn's moon Mimas has a distinctive feature which has a diameter almost one-third of Mimas' diameter. What is it?
   a) A giant impact crater
   b) A giant lake
   c) A giant alien spaceship

8. Titania is the largest moon of which planet?
   a) Pluto
   b) Uranus
   c) Saturn

9. How many known moons does the planet Neptune have?
   a) 0
   b) 14
   c) 74

10. Which of these statements about Charon, the largest moon of Pluto, is true?
    a) It is very large in comparison to the size of Pluto
    b) It is actually bigger than Pluto
    c) It is the smallest known moon in the Solar System

Word wheels

Can you work out the moons in the three word wheels?
See if you are right by flicking to page 99.

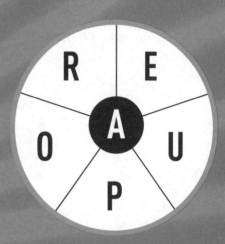

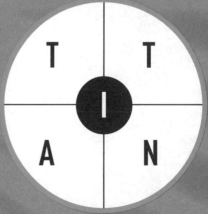

Stars and Constellations

Read on for fun facts and puzzles on stars and constellations.

No-one knows who **FIRST CHARTED** the **CONSTELLATIONS** but it is thought to have been the **SUMERIANS** or **BABYLONIANS, 4000 YEARS AGO!**

STARS AND CONSTELLATIONS

Stars are big, bright, exploding balls of gas in the sky. The closest star to Earth is the Sun. On clear nights, many other stars can be seen twinkling in the sky.

Groups of stars that make imaginary shapes in the sky are called constellations. Often, they are named after mythological characters or animals.

HERCULES is a constellation named after the **ROMAN HERO** and **GOD** Hercules. He was knows as **HERACLES** in **GREEK** mythology and was son of **ZEUS.**

CROSSWORDS

Solve the cryptic clues below to turn the telescope to the Plough.
Answers have the same amount of letters as the number in brackets.
Can you work out the stars and constellations keyword using the letters in
the shaded squares? See if you are right by flicking to page 100.

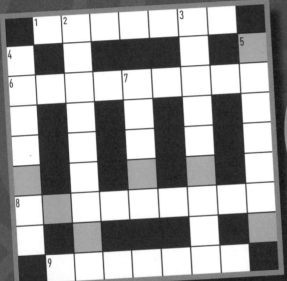

100,000 YEARS from now, the constellations we know will look very different. Because of how we move through space, **SCIENTISTS** predict that one day the **BIG DIPPER** will look more like a **BIG DUCK!**

Across

1 Opposite of public (7)
6 Building designer (9)
8 A legendary story usually for children (5,4)
9 Not fortunate (7)

Down

2 Entrance area of a hotel (9)
3 Place with rides and fun things to do (5,4)
4 Capital city of Wales (7)
5 First course of a meal (7)
7 Country where one finds Rome (5)

Across

4 Dad (6)
6 You use these to hear (4)
7 Zeus and Aries are these (4)
8 Opposite of home (4)
9 An edible seed (4)
10 Split into smaller parts (6)

Down

1 The night of 31 October (9)
2 Ten lots of one hundred (8)
3 You might spread this on toast (9)
5 A sister or uncle, for instance (8)

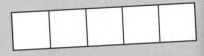

You may have heard of the **Plough** before, also known as the **Big Dipper,** but did you know that it belongs to a larger constellation? It forms part of **Ursa Major,** commonly known as the **Great Bear.** The handle of the Plough represents the bear's tail – even though bears don't really have tails!

The Plough

SUDOKUS

Solve the sudokus to make Polaris sparkle.
Fill in the blank squares so that numbers 1 to 6 appear once in each row,
column and 3x2 box. See if you are right by flicking to page 100.

Ursa Minor is
another name for the
constellation known as the
Little Bear. Just as
the Big Dipper forms the
Great Bear's tail, the
Little Dipper forms
the Little Bear's tail! The
brightest star in Ursa
Minor is **Polaris,**
Earth's north celestial
pole.

		6		4	
	3				
			3	5	
3	2	5			4
				1	
	6		4		

			3		
2	3	5	4		1
1					
					2
		2	6	1	
		3			

Wordsearches

Search the Solar Sytem to find the star-related terms.
Look left to right, up and down to find the words listed in the boxes below.
See if you are right by flicking to page 100.

i	x	t	u	l	i	g	h	t	u
a	h	f	s	b	j	h	b	z	r
p	a	u	u	t	a	u	r	u	s
r	p	a	n	n	r	o	g	c	a
p	e	r	s	e	u	s	a	j	m
i	g	h	p	r	c	s	k	t	a
s	a	e	o	r	i	o	n	k	j
c	s	a	t	t	r	i	w	g	o
e	u	t	k	c	t	u	t	x	r
s	s	i	r	i	u	s	i	h	a

- heat
- light
- Orion
- Pegasus
- Perseus
- Pisces
- Sirius
- sunspot
- Taurus
- Ursa Major

Sirius is the brightest star in the night sky, which is why its name comes from a Greek word meaning 'glowing' or 'scorching'. It can also be known as the **Dog Star,** because it forms part of **Canis Major** – a constellation which is said to

l	a	a	u	s	m	l	u	b	s
z	a	r	i	e	s	e	r	e	a
h	e	r	c	u	l	e	s	t	n
s	s	a	g	i	t	t	a	e	d
d	m	u	e	s	e	t	m	l	r
r	o	r	m	i	o	p	i	g	o
a	c	i	i	q	b	i	n	e	m
c	y	g	n	u	s	r	o	u	e
o	a	a	i	y	g	o	r	s	d
i	i	t	t	i	l	a	t	e	a

Andromeda
Aries
Auriga
Betelgeuse
Cygnus
Draco
Gemini
Hercules
Sagitta
Ursa Minor

SIRIUS is so far away, it takes light from the star over **EIGHT YEARS** to reach us.

Canis Major

MAZES

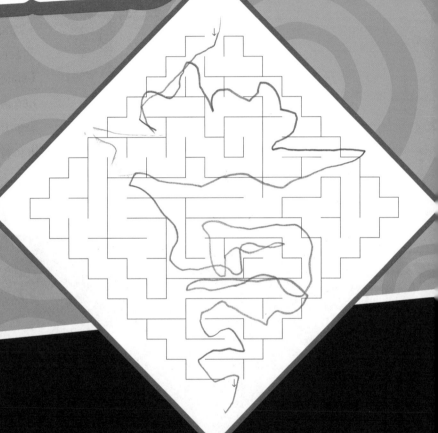

Follow the light of Betelgeuse around the maze until you reach the exit. See if you are right by flicking to page 101.

Orion is a distinctive constellation that is known by many cultures around the world and has lots of different myths associated with it. Orion's brightest stars are **Rigel,** which looks like one star from Earth but is actually made up of a number of stars, and **Betelgeuse,** which is a red supergiant

Orion

GUESS WHAT?

Can you guess the answers to the stars and constellations questions below?
Check your guesses by flicking to page 101.

1. What is the name of the star closest to our planet?
   a) Vega
   b) Sun
   c) Procyon

2. A star shines by fusing hydrogen into which other element in its core?
   a) Copper
   b) Gold
   c) Helium

3. When a massive star collapses at the end of its life cycle, it might form which of these?
   a) Yellow hole
   b) Blue hole
   c) Black hole

4. What is the name of the brightest star in the night sky?
   a) Sirius
   b) Aquarius
   c) Serious

5. What is the name of the second-brightest star in the night sky?
   a) Octopus
   b) Tinopus
   c) Canopus

6. Rigel is the brightest star in which constellation?
   a) Onion
   b) Ocean
   c) Orion

7. Which of these is the name of a constellation?
   a) Andromeda
   b) Butdromeda
   c) Alsodromeda

8. What is another name of the constellation Ursa Major?
   a) Great Chair
   b) Great Bear
   c) Great Stair

9. What name is given to a famous pattern formed by seven bright stars in Ursa Major?
   a) The Brow
   b) The Plough
   c) The Cow

10. Leo is a constellation. Its name is Latin for:
    a) Lion
    b) Tiger
    c) Bear

Word wheels

Can you work out the star words in the three word wheels?
See if you are right by flicking to page 101.

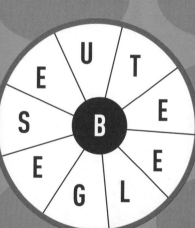

Space Exploration and History

Eager to learn about space exploration? Read on for fun facts and puzzles.

The

HUBBLE SPACE TELESCOPE

has captured a photo that peers

13.2 BILLION YEARS

into the Universe's past; that's as far as we will ever see.

SPACE
EXPLORATION

1957	The first artificial satellite, Sputnik 1, launched
1959	First photograph of Earth from orbit
1961	First man in space
1963	First woman in space
1965	First images of Mars
1965	First space walk
1966	First spacecraft to land on the Moon
1969	Man lands on the Moon

1957 to 1969

1970 to 1979

1970	First lunar rover
1971	First space station
1972	Last man on the moon
1973	First images of Jupiter
1974	First images of Venus
1977	Voyager spacecrafts launched
1979	First images of Jupiter and Saturn

For decades, humans have been trying to find out more about what goes on in our Solar System. Space shuttles, astronauts, artificial satellites and many more forms of technology have been used to explore and discover outer space.

Mark the milestones using the timeline below.

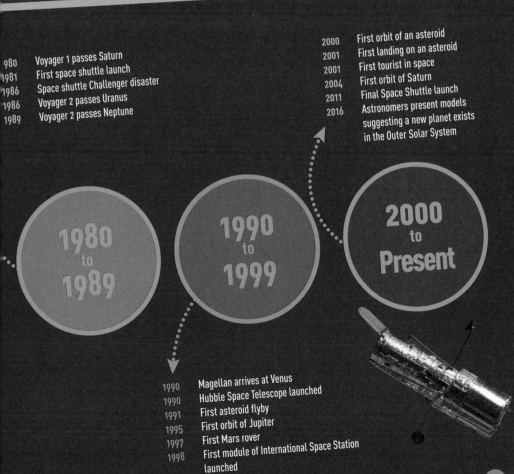

1980   Voyager 1 passes Saturn
1981   First space shuttle launch
1986   Space shuttle Challenger disaster
1986   Voyager 2 passes Uranus
1989   Voyager 2 passes Neptune

2000   First orbit of an asteroid
2001   First landing on an asteroid
2001   First tourist in space
2004   First orbit of Saturn
2011   Final Space Shuttle launch
2016   Astronomers present models
        suggesting a new planet exists
        in the Outer Solar System

1980
to
1989

1990
to
1999

2000
to
Present

1990   Magellan arrives at Venus
1990   Hubble Space Telescope launched
1991   First asteroid flyby
1995   First orbit of Jupiter
1997   First Mars rover
1998   First module of International Space Station
        launched

CROSSWORDS

Help the astronauts crack the crosswords by solving the cryptic clues below. Answers have the same amount of letters as the number in brackets. Can you work out the space exploration keyword using the letters in the shaded squares? See if you are right by flicking to page 102.

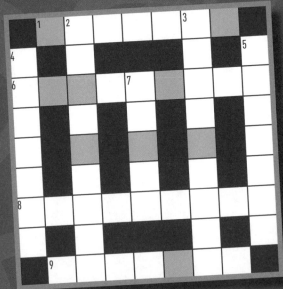

The first two dogs to make a return **FLIGHT** to space were Belka and Strelka; they went to **SPACE** for a day in **1960** before safely returning to **EARTH.**

Across

1 Country where you find New York (7)
6 Amuse (9)
8 Time when you are young (9)
9 Greet (7)

Down

2 A two-wheeled vehicle with an engine (9)
3 Place in a school where lessons take place (9)
4 Bird with impressive tail feathers (7)
5 Contain as part of a whole (7)
7 Circular (5)

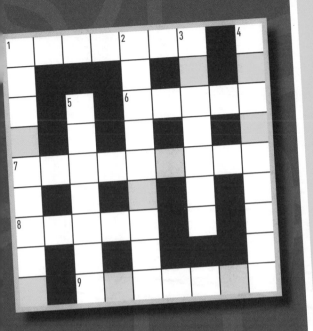

An **astronaut** is a person who travels into space. The first person in space was Yuri Gagarin, a Russian astronaut who made a 108-minute space shuttle flight in 1961. Valentina Tereshkova was the first woman in space; in 1963 she spent three days there, orbiting Earth 48 times!

Across

1 Opposite of analogue (7)
6 Bitter-tasting substances (5)
7 Your way of writing your name (9)
8 Suing (anag.) (5)
9 This starts a tennis point (7)

Down

1 Extinct animals that were often huge (9)
2 ___ Square: London tourist attraction (9)
3 Free time (7)
4 Having a great desire for something (9)
5 Black-and-white crows with long tails (7)

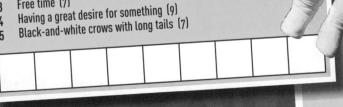

SUDOKUS

Solve the sudokus to launch the space shuttle. Fill in the blank squares so that numbers 1 to 6 appear once in each row, column and 3x2 box. See if you are right by flicking to page 102.

Up to six people can **LIVE** in the International **SPACE STATION.** It is as **BIG** as a six-bedroom house, has two bathrooms, many science labs, and even a **GYM!**

1	5				
3				4	
		6		2	
	3			6	
	2				3
				1	6

2			1		4
		1			5
				1	
	6				2
4			2		3
3		5			1

The first **space shuttle launch** in 1981 was the beginning of a new era for space travel. Space shuttles take off like rockets, but land like planes, so they are much more reusable. In 1998, the **International Space Station** was launched, which is a large home for astronauts that orbits the Earth.

85

Wordsearches

Search the Solar Sytem to find the space words. Look left to right,
up and down to find the words listed in the boxes below.
See if you are right by flicking to page 102.

astronaut
galaxy
Hubble
lunar rover
Milky Way
satellites
shuttle
space suit
space walk
Voyager

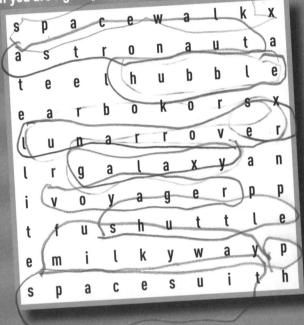

```
s p a c e w a l k x
a s t r o n a u t a
t e e l h u b b l e
e a r b o k o r s x
l u n a r r o v e r
l r g a l a x y a n
i v o y a g e r p p
t f u s h u t t l e
e m i l k y w a y p
s p a c e s u i t h
```

Rovers are special robotic vehicles designed to explore the surfaces of other planets. They don't need to have people in them, so they can go to faraway places like Mars.

Satellites are used to observe planets from orbit. They don't need to land, so they can explore planets that are even further away, like Uranus and Neptune.

f	l	y	b	y	s	o	y	m	j
a	q	s	u	l	c	t	y	o	o
h	m	o	d	u	l	e	s	o	g
a	m	a	g	e	l	l	a	n	o
p	p	h	i	l	a	e	u	f	q
o	j	q	c	a	s	s	i	n	i
l	w	n	b	i	e	c	s	e	v
l	m	a	r	s	r	o	v	e	r
o	s	x	a	g	s	p	j	l	u
e	g	a	l	i	l	e	o	t	v

Apollo
Cassini
flyby
Galileo
Magellan
Mars rover
module
moon
Philae
telescope

In **2012,** a spacecraft called **VOYAGER 1** officially became the first human-made object to leave our **SOLAR SYSTEM.** It is now in interstellar space, over **21,000,000,000 KILOMETRES** from **EARTH** – and still going!

Compare the two images of the astronaut.
Can you spot the five differences between the images?
See if you are right by flicking to page 103.

See if you are right by flicking to page 103.

PILOTS
must have at least 1000
HOURS OF FLYING
experience before they
can apply to be an
ASTRONAUT.

CLOSE UP

Match the mind-boggling magnifications to the named pictures opposite.
See if you are right by flicking to page 103.

1

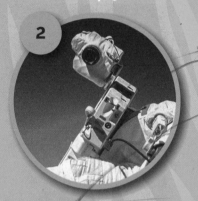

2

3

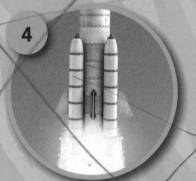

4

5

6

Rover

1

Hubble Telescope

2

Space station

3

Astronaut

4

Space shuttle

5

Rocket

6

GUESS WHAT?

Can you guess the answers to the space exploration questions below?
Check your guesses by flicking to page 103.

1. Who is famously associated with the telescope?
   a) Galileo
   b) Euclid
   c) Socrates

2. Which of these is the name of a famous telescope?
   a) Bubble Space Telescope
   b) Hubble Space Telescope
   c) Rubble Space Telescope

3. What was the first planet discovered with a telescope?
   a) Jupiter
   b) Saturn
   c) Uranus

4. In which year did humans first land on the Moon?
   a) 1949
   b) 1969
   c) 1989

5. What was the name of the first artificial satellite launched?
   a) Spacenik 1
   b) Robotnik 1
   c) Sputnik 1

6. What is the name of a person who goes into space?
   a) Braveonaut
   b) Staronaut
   c) Astronaut

7. Who was the first person to walk on the Moon?
   a) Neil Aldrin
   b) Neil Collins
   c) Neil Armstrong

8. What is the name of the artificial satellite in low Earth orbit that is visited by astronauts?
   a) Multinational Space Station
   b) Supernational Space Station
   c) International Space Station

9. Which of these is the name of a rover exploring Mars?
   a) Curiosity
   b) Boredom
   c) Indifference

10. Which hugely successful space mission to Saturn ended in September 2017 with the probe intentionally destroying itself?
    a) Mir
    b) Skylab
    c) Cassini

Word wheels

Can you work out the space exploration words in the three word wheels?
See if you are right by flicking to page 103.

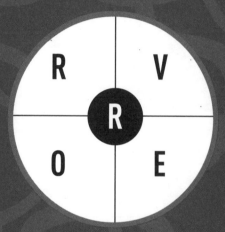

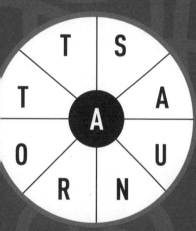

Solutions

Page 12–13

Crosswords

Keyword: PLANETS

Keyword: MERCURY

Page 14–15

Sudokus

2	4	6	3	1	5
1	5	3	4	6	2
4	1	2	6	5	3
6	3	5	2	4	1
3	6	1	5	2	4
5	2	4	1	3	6

3	2	6	4	5	1
4	5	1	3	6	2
6	3	2	5	1	4
1	4	5	6	2	3
5	1	3	2	4	6
2	6	4	1	3	5

Page 16–17

Wordsearches

Page 18–19

Word jumbles

1) Atmosphere
2) Oceans
3) Gravity
4) Mantle
5) Crust

94

ASTEROID BELT

EARTH

Solutions

Crosswords

Page 34–35

Grid 1:

```
H I G H L I G H T
E   A         I   A
D I P   A R     R   R
G   S O M A L I A   N
E       A           T
H O R I Z O N       T
O       E     E M U L
        M     M     L
S U P E R N O V A
```

Keyword: SATURN

Grid 2:

```
E M E R G E N C Y
X   G         I   E
P I G     A   C   S
E   S U G G E S T
N     R           E
S U B J E C T     R
I   O   E     R E D
V   O         E   A
E X T R E M E L Y
```

Keyword: JUPITER

Sudokus

Page 36–37

4	2	1	5	6	3
3	6	5	2	4	1
2	3	4	1	5	6
5	1	6	4	3	2
6	5	2	3	1	4
1	4	3	6	2	5

5	3	1	2	6	4
4	6	2	3	1	5
2	4	6	1	5	3
1	5	3	4	2	6
6	2	4	5	3	1
3	1	5	6	4	2

Wordsearches

Page 38–39

```
q m h o s s u s g u
i o u j r a r e w w
l o g u k t a r t k
q n e p t u n e i g
t s r i l r u d u s
o n i t l n s s u e
s r n e w p e p n t
z f g r p p c o l d
g a s g i a n t s n
o r y e x s i z r i
```

```
w p s i a p e t u s
r p e c a t h e b e
z l s h b r y b t j
p b c a i s p u i p
h y d r o g e n t l
o p j o o m r o a u
e b q n l i i o n t
b f s l r m o b i o
e z m i r a n d a o
l v w e k s v u l f
```

Page 40-41 Mazes

Page 42-43 Word jumbles

1) Dwarf   2) Asteroids   3) Jupiter   4) Jovian   5) Uranus

Page 44-45 Codewords

KUIPER BELT   NEPTUNE

Page 46-47 Close up

1 – 5 Pluto
2 – 3 Uranus
3 – 2 Saturn
4 – 1 Jupiter
5 – 4 Neptune

Page 48-49 Guess what?

1) b – Gas Giants
3) c – Great Red Spot
5) c – Ganymede
7) b – Titan
9) a – The Roman god of the sea

2) a – Saturn
4) c – More than 60
6) b – Hydrogen
8) a – Uranus
10) a – Pluto

Word wheels

Neptune   Jupiter   Saturn

Solutions

Page 54–55

Crosswords

Crossword 1:

W	E	D	N	E	S	D	A	Y	
E					T		E		
S	U	P	P	O	R	T		A	
T		R			E			R	
	W	H	I	S	T	L	E		
N		V		C			H		
A		M	A	C	H	I	N	E	
S		T					R		
A	D	V	E	N	T	U	R	E	

Keyword: SEASON

Crossword 2:

	W		C				M		
M	E	T	H	O	D		A		
	D		I		E	A	R	S	
	N		L		S		M		
M	E	N	D		C	H	A	T	
	S		R		R		L		
E	D	G	E		I		A		
	A		N	O	B	O	D	Y	
	Y				E		E		

Keyword: GANYMEDE

Page 56–57

Sudokus

Sudoku 1:

3	4	1	6	5	2
5	2	6	4	3	1
6	3	2	1	4	5
1	5	4	2	6	3
2	6	5	3	1	4
4	1	3	5	2	6

Sudoku 2:

1	5	2	6	3	4
6	4	3	5	2	1
4	6	1	3	5	2
2	3	5	1	4	6
5	1	4	2	6	3
3	2	6	4	1	5

Page 58–59

Wordsearches

Mazes

Guess what?

1) b – 2
2) c – About 4.5 billion years ago
3) b – About 27 days
4) a – Io
5) a – Europa
6) a – Rhea
7) a – A giant impact crater
8) b – Uranus
9) b – 14
10) a – It is very large in comparison to the size of Pluto

Word wheels

Europa   Deimos   Titan

Solutions

Crosswords

Crossword 1:

	P	R	I	V	A	T	E	
C		E			H		S	
A	R	C	H	I	T	E	C	T
R		E		T		M		A
D		P		A		E		R
I		T		L		P		T
F	A	I	R	Y	T	A	L	E
F		O				R		R
	U	N	L	U	C	K	Y	

Keyword: POLARIS

Crossword 2:

	H		T				M		
F	A	T	H	E	R		A	R	
	L		O		E	A	R	S	
	L		U		L		M		
G	O	D	S		A	W	A	Y	
	W		A		T		L	A	
B	E	A	N		I		A		
	E		D	I	V	I	D	E	
	N				E		E		

Keyword: LIGHT

Sudokus

Sudoku 1:

2	1	6	5	4	3
5	3	4	6	2	1
6	4	1	3	5	2
3	2	5	1	6	4
4	5	3	2	1	6
1	6	2	4	3	5

Sudoku 2:

4	6	1	3	2	5
2	3	5	4	6	1
1	2	4	5	3	6
3	5	6	1	4	2
5	4	2	6	1	3
6	1	3	2	5	4

Wordsearches

Wordsearch 1:

i	x	t	u	l	i	g	h	t	u
a	h	f	s	b	j	h	b	z	r
p	a	u	u	t	a	u	r	u	s
r	p	a	n	n	r	o	g	c	a
p	e	r	s	e	u	s	a	j	m
i	g	h	p	r	c	s	k	t	a
s	a	e	o	r	i	o	n	k	j
c	s	a	t	t	r	i	w	g	o
e	u	t	k	c	t	u	t	x	r
s	s	s	i	r	i	u	s	i	h	a

Wordsearch 2:

l	a	a	u	s	m	l	u	b	s
z	a	r	i	e	s	e	r	e	a
h	e	r	c	u	l	e	s	t	n
s	s	a	g	i	t	t	a	e	d
d	m	u	e	s	e	t	m	l	r
r	o	r	m	i	o	p	i	g	o
a	c	i	i	q	b	i	n	e	m
c	y	g	n	u	s	r	o	u	e
o	a	a	i	y	g	o	r	s	d
i	i	t	t	i	l	a	t	e	

Mazes

Guess what?

1) b – Sun
2) c – Helium
3) c – Black hole
4) a – Sirius
5) c – Canopus
6) c – Orion
7) a – Andromeda
8) b – Great Bear
9) b – The Plough
10) a – Lion

Word wheels

Orion

Betelgeuse

Sirius

Solutions

Page 82–83

Crosswords

Keyword: ASTRONAUT

Keyword: TELESCOPE

Page 84–85

Sudokus

1	5	4	6	3	2
3	6	2	5	4	1
4	1	6	3	2	5
2	3	5	1	6	4
6	2	1	4	5	3
5	4	3	2	1	6

2	5	3	1	6	4
6	4	1	3	2	5
5	3	2	4	1	6
1	6	4	5	3	2
4	1	6	2	5	3
3	2	5	6	4	1

Page 86–87

Wordsearches

Page 88–89

Spot the difference

Page 90–91

Close up

1 – 5 Space shuttle   2 – 4 Astronaut   3 – 3 Space station
4 – 6 Rocket   5 – 1 Rover   6 – 2 Hubble Telescope

Page 92–93

Guess what?

1) a – Galileo   2) b – Hubble Space Telescope
3) c – Uranus   4) b – 1969
5) c – Sputnik 1   6) c – Astronaut
7) c – Neil Armstrong   8) c – International Space Station
9) a – Curiosity   10) c – Cassini

Word wheels

Rover   Astronaut   Telescope